better together*

*This book is best read together, grownup and kid.

akidsco.com

a kids book about

a kids book about

donor conceived people

— by Taylor Hovish

a kids book about

Text and design copyright © 2024
by A Kids Book About, Inc.

Copyright is good! It ensures that work like this can exist, and more work in the future can be created.

All rights reserved. No part of this publication may be reproduced, distributed, or transmitted in any form or by any means, including photocopying, recording, other electronic or mechanical methods, without the prior written permission of the publisher, except in the case of brief quotations embodied in critical reviews and certain other noncommercial uses permitted by copyright law. For permission requests, write to the publisher.

A Kids Book About, Kids Are Ready, and the colophon 'a' are trademarks of A Kids Book About, Inc.

Printed in the United States of America.

A Kids Book About books are available online: *akidsco.com*

To share your stories, ask questions, or inquire about bulk purchases (schools, libraries, and nonprofits), please use the following email address: *hello@akidsco.com*

Print ISBN: 979-8-89281-038-8
Ebook ISBN: 979-8-89281-039-5

Designed by Jelani Memory
Edited by Emma Wolf

For my mom, Patricia, and my husband, Mike, who are always my greatest supporters.

And for all my own donor siblings—Devon, Kylee, Rachel, Hillary, Sara, and Whitney—who have added so much joy and love to my life.

Intro

Creation stories—every culture has them. From gods giving light to the universe, to Earth forming on the backs of giant creatures, humanity has been trying to answer the question, "Where did we come from?" since the beginning of time. It makes sense, then, for our kids to wonder about how they came to be. Everyone has the right to know their personal origin story. And the cool part is, each of us has a special story!

This is a book about my journey as a donor conceived person and the impact it has had on my life. If you love a donor conceived person, I hope this book helps you understand the unique joys, challenges, and questions they may face. If you are a donor conceived person, I hope this book helps you embrace your special origin story!

Hi! I'm Taylor. And this is a book about

donor conceived people.

What does that mean?

Well, I'll explain it to you!

Gametes (ga-meets) are the cells in our bodies that can make babies.

There are 2 types of gametes, sperm cells and egg cells.

Sometimes, gametes from someone other than the parent are used to conceive a baby.

(Conceive is just another way of saying make.)

And this could be for different reasons!

Someone who gives their gametes to other people to help them have a baby is called a **donor**.

Doctors can use donor sperm cells, donor egg cells, or both!

And babies who are made using gametes from a donor are called **donor conceived people**.

Are you with me so far?

I know a lot about this because
I'm a donor conceived person.

And maybe you are too!
Or maybe you know someone
who is a donor conceived person.

When my mom decided she wanted to have a baby, her doctor used sperm from a donor combined with my mom's egg to conceive me.

When doctors use donor gametes, there are several ways the sperm and egg can combine to make a baby.

Sometimes a doctor inserts the donor cells into the birthing person's body, and the baby is conceived there.

Other times the sperm and the egg are combined outside the body.

The cells grow into an embryo* and then a doctor transfers the embryo into the birthing person's body, where it grows into a baby.

*An embryo is an initial stage of development for new life.

Growing up, my mom made sure I knew how I was conceived and how loved I was.

It wasn't just 1 conversation we had and then moved on from.

We kept a continual, open dialogue so I could ask questions and she could share honestly with me.

Maybe you have some questions about donor conceived people too!

If you are a donor conceived person, maybe you're curious...

How did my grownup choose the donor?

Do they know who the donor is?

Am I like the donor?

How do I talk about this with other people?

It's natural to wonder about these things.

If you are a donor conceived person, a big thing I want you to know is

you're not alone.

You're not the only person with questions.

And it's important to have the answers you're looking for.

When I was a kid, I didn't know any other donor conceived people.

While I loved my family,
I sometimes felt confused.

As I got older, I started to wonder what else I didn't know about myself or my family.

So, I decided to dive deeper into my origin story—the story of me!

Through DNA* testing, I found out more about my ancestry.**

*DNA is found in your body's cells and gives you the traits that make you who you are.

**Someone's ancestry is the story of where their family is from and the people who came before them.

It turns out, other families used sperm from the same donor my mom chose.

I grew up an only child, but through this journey, I discovered I actually have a lot of biological siblings!

This changed what I understood about myself.

I had never been a sister before!

And meeting my donor siblings as a grownup was a unique experience.

We didn't grow up in the same house, and we don't have the same mom.

Even still, when I first met each of them, I felt an instant connection.

I feel really happy to have these relationships.

confused surprised disappointed enthusiastic ins
self-conscious vulnerable fortunate proud con
joy affection compassion powerless empowered
glad hopeful appreciated confident determin
fulfilled grateful dejected empty ashamed d
agitated betrayed hesitant puzzled uncertain

This is *my* story as a donor conceived person, but each person's story is unique.

stagnant flustered misunderstood torn unde
frantic defensive concerned directionless fear
excited furious cheated energized confused surp
concerned optimistic frustrated isolated grief re
hopeful alive cheerful delighted fortunate go
dejected empty ashamed disappointed exhaus

curious indifferent grateful overwhelmed alone
optimistic frustrated isolated grief relieved
eful alive cheerful delighted ecstatic flattered
rtunate good joyful assured content elated
inted exhausted frustrated enraged displeased
tracted foggy doubtful ambivalent bothered

And each story comes with LOTS of different feelings.

uncomfortable surprised impatient insecure
nxious alarmed intimidated shaken reluctant
disappointed enthusiastic insecure curious proud
joy affection compassion powerless empowered
yful assured content elated fulfilled grateful
frustrated enraged displeased great guarded

Whatever feelings you may have are totally OK and yours to feel.

Some of my siblings weren't sure what to think when we first connected.

And others could not have been more excited!

The journey of being a donor conceived person is super **personal**, **emotional**, and **unique** to each individual.

In developing relationships with each of my siblings, I've learned that *consent* is an important part of this experience.

Every donor conceived person has their own **boundaries**, **preferences**, and **comfort zone** when it comes to exploring their identity.

For me, I was excited to get to know my siblings and build connections, but I'm not interested in knowing my donor.

My life feels *complete*

the way it is!

But if knowing your donor feels important to you, you have every right to talk to your grownups about learning more.

They might not have all the answers to your questions, and that's OK.

If you are a donor conceived person,

I hope you embrace
your unique origin story.

Being a donor conceived person is...

So cool.

You were so thoughtfully created,

and your beginnings are

If you want to support a donor conceived person, create a safe space for them to ask questions and share their journey.

Above all, approach conversations with curiosity and openness!

When you meet someone new, learn about their family and leave your assumptions behind.

Damselflies with adventures of different days

So, what do you want to share about your origin story?

These are good resources for donor conceived people, their families, and anyone interested in learning more:

**wearedonorconceived.com • usdcc.org
donorsiblingregistry.com**

Outro

Thank you for reading my story! I hope this book leads to thoughtful questions and powerful conversations. I know those discussions can sometimes feel too big. Too complicated. Too emotional. But that's OK! Kids are ready to explore big, complicated, and emotional topics.

An important thing I want you to know is that donor conceived kids may have unique challenges with how they understand their identity and how they navigate relationships. They may not always have words to describe their origin, but one of the best things you can do is listen. More and more donor conceived babies are born every year. There could be a donor conceived person in your life and you may not even know it! So please always be aware of the assumptions you might be making about someone's story.

Now, it's time to celebrate your own family's origins!

About The Author

Taylor Hovish (she/her) wanted to write the book she wished she had growing up as a donor conceived person. As a kid, she didn't know any other donor conceived people and she struggled to find the words to explain her origin story.

The unique experience of finding and meeting siblings as a grownup inspired her to become more involved in the wider donor conceived community. She is a strong supporter of initiatives that protect the health and wellbeing of all future donor conceived people, such as verifying donor medical history and prohibiting donor anonymity. She hopes this book helps kids feel more understood and helps grownups feel more comfortable talking about this topic.

If you'd like to share your own origin story, or just chat, you can email her at taylorhovish@gmail.com.

 @akidsco  @akidsco  akidsco.com

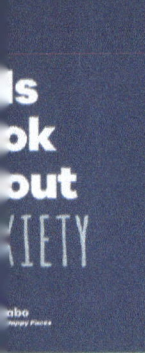   

Discover more at akidsco.com

www.ingramcontent.com/pod-product-compliance
Lightning Source LLC
Chambersburg PA
CBHW061359010526
44107CB00012B/984